To
LESLIE,
best wishes,
Sandoval.

DIZZY GILLESPIE
THE MAN WHO CHANGED MY LIFE

From the Memoirs of
Arturo Sandoval

Also available from GIA Publications, Inc., by Robert Simon;
Fennell: A Tribute to Frederick Fennell (G-6532)
Percy Grainger: The Pictorial Biography (G-6583)

Robert Simon
and Marianela Sandoval

foreword by
Quincy Jones

DIZZY GILLESPIE
THE MAN WHO CHANGED MY LIFE

From the Memoirs of
Arturo Sandoval

GIA Publications Inc.

NATIONS HIGHEST CIVILIAN HONOR AWARDED TO ARTURO SANDOVAL

THE PRESIDENTIAL MEDAL OF FREEDOM
NOVEMBER, 2013

"I feel overwhelmed by the Presidential Medal of Freedom. It's an immense honor for me and I strongly believe Freedom is the most important thing in life, God Bless the USA!"

— Arturo Sandoval

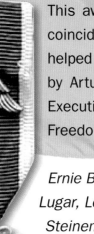

This award could not have come at a more poignant time in Arturo's life. It coincides with the release of this book hallmarking the freedom Dizzy Gillespie helped Arturo achieve as well as the celebration of 50 years of music making by Arturo Sandoval. This same year also marks the 50th anniversary of the Executive Order signed by President John F Kennedy establishing this Medal of Freedom Award. Fellow recipients of this prestigious award in 2013 include:

Ernie Banks, Ben Bradlee, Bill Clinton, Daniel Inouye, Daniel Kahneman, Richard Lugar, Loretta Lynn, Mario Molina, Sally Ride, Bayard Rustin, Dean Smith, Gloria Steinem, C.T. Vivian, Patricia Wald and Oprah Winfrey.

The award is bestowed by the President of the United States and recognizes special individuals who have made "an especially meritorious contribution to the security of national interests of the United States, world peace, cultural or other significant public or private endeavors".

Acknowledgments

- Leonid Afremov
- Shelly Berg
- Jeanie Bryson
- City of Cheraw, SC
- Bill Cosby
- Downbeat Collection
  (The Library of Congress)
- Downbeat Magazine Archives
- Svein E. Furulund
- Andy Garcia
- GIA Publications
- Dany Gignoux
- Roland Godefroy
- William Gottlieb Collection
  (The Library of Congress)

- Alec Harris
- Slide Hampton
- Quincy Jones
- Charles "The Whale" Lake
- Library of Congress
- Frank Martin
- Frank "Bishop" McDuffie
  (Lauringburg Institute of Music)
- Rob Miseur
- Joe Pesci
- Marc Pokempner
- Uli Pschewschny
- Poncho Sanchez
- Loras Schissel

- Ronnie Scott's Jazz Club
- Ned Sublette
- The Berlin Club
- The Blue Note Club
- The Simon Family
- The Village Gate
- Barry Thomson
- Dello Valdes
- Frank Vardaros
- Carl Van Vechten Collection
  (The Library of Congress)
- Darron Walsh

Publication layout and design by:
Darron Walsh
Principal, Visual Viewpoint

ARTURO
SANDOVAL

Table of Contents

Foreword

by Quincy Jones

Divine intervention is often what brings greatness to a musician's ability to play his instrument. However, it is passion—that is, the magic—that transcends mere mortals. The passion of a man and his instrument, the passion of a composer and his composition, and the passion that binds all of us in this very special love affair we have with music.

Such a passion existed between two great artists, Dizzy Gillespie and Arturo Sandoval. From the time they met, the magic flowed…from the charts they wrote, to the horns they played, to the time their families spent together.

This book is an intimate and unique peek inside the personal life and times of these two men, their careers, and their families. I feel truly honored and blessed to have worked with each of these multi-generational talents. They touch my heart deeply. I love Dizzy and Arturo, and consider them both as my "forever" friends and brothers. Share, with me, this very candid look at three decades of music, two giants of music, and one beautiful friendship.

In Oslo, Norway, 1991. Photo by Svein E. Furulund.

Introduction

It was an amazing honor when Arturo and Marianela invited me to collaborate with them on their tribute to Dizzy Gillespie. This was a comprehensive project that encompassed the writing of this book, the recording of the phenomenal new "DEAR DIZ" CD (which earned Arturo his ninth Grammy Award), the potential of a television special and documentary, an extensive concert tour honoring Dizzy's work, and finally, a major tribute concert honoring 50 years of the music of Arturo Sandoval.

Throughout his career, Dizzy faced a huge challenge to achieve success as a black man born in the South with limited education. He endured the hardship of the Great Depression as well as the humiliation and restrictions of the deep-rooted racism and segregation of the time. The dream of a musical career represented Dizzy's escape from the oppression he experienced in the South.

Decades later, Arturo suffered his own bonds of tyranny when he was forbidden the freedom to perform the music he loved. While serving his three years of obligatory military service in Cuba, he was jailed for three months for listening to the "Voice of America" program hosted by Willis Conover on a short wave radio. Both Dizzy and Arturo were angered and demoralized by their individual circumstances, yet both found ways to persevere no matter the political or social consequences of the times.

Arturo and Rob Simon in rehearsal at Wake Forest University. Photo by Kevin Slusher.

Early in his career, Dizzy made his way to New York City, where he struggled to earn enough to subsist. In New York he met Mario Bauzá, and his life and career began to change. Mario was a major figure in Dizzy's life, and he became instrumental in Dizzy's eventual breakthrough and success by providing exceptional opportunities at the perfect times. Once Dizzy had performance traction, there was no looking back.

There is an astounding parallel between the relationship of Mario Bauzá and Dizzy, and later, the relationship of Dizzy and Arturo. Mario Bauzá, considered by his colleagues

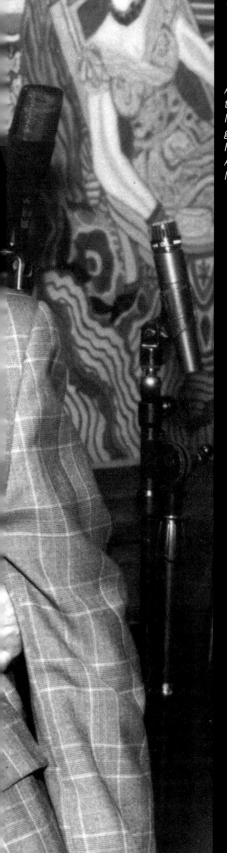

Auturo and Mario Bauzá in 1991 - from the front cover of Downbeat Magazine. Mario was instrumental in helping Dizzy get gigs early on and later introduced him to Chano Pozo. Dizzy also introduced Arturo to Mario. Courtesy of Downbeat Magazine

as the father of Latin jazz, was a prodigy clarinet player, classically trained in Havana, who loved and understood American jazz. In 1930, Bauzá arrived in New York and quickly switched from the clarinet to the trumpet, leaving the classical music scene behind and embarking upon a career that would span over seven decades. During this time he played in the best jazz bands as a section player and soloist and was bandleader of his own groups, composer, and teacher. Mario Bauzá intervened in Dizzy's life and career at just the right time, just as Dizzy would later intercede in Arturo's. Dizzy's assistance and encouragement were crucial to Arturo's variety of musical opportunities and his eventual flight to freedom.

One does not have to look far to realize the level of affection that quickly grew between Dizzy Gillespie and Arturo Sandoval. Their relationship was not only one of mentor-protégé, but also a father-son type of kinship. Dizzy never had a son until he met Arturo. In video footage and many still pictures, it is apparent that Dizzy felt Arturo was more than just another musician playing a gig; he treated Arturo with great fondness, always expressing genuine admiration and support.

There is no doubt that Dizzy took pride in encouraging Arturo to pursue his thoughts and dreams. He assisted and supported Arturo in multiple break-through gigs and recordings. However, beyond the music, there is also the wonderful human story of how Dizzy helped facilitate the defection of Arturo, Marianela, and Tury from Cuba.

Who knows where Dizzy's life and career may have ended up had it not been for the intervention of Mario Bauzá. As fate would have it, the same could be asked of Arturo, had it not been for Dizzy's remarkable timing. I discussed this with Arturo, and his immediate response was the rhetorical question: "Why do you think I am calling this book *The Man Who Changed My Life*? Maybe I would have ended up in jail, or worse, because nothing good could have happened to me if I stayed there." Obviously, all of these musicians rank in the very top of their field and we know that something amazing was in store for each of them. It was a matter of timing, opportunity, being prepared, and seizing the moment.

Four times during the past decade I have been on stage with Arturo Sandoval, conducting classical concertos and scintillating jazz charts. As you can imagine, it was a mind-jolting and artistically life-changing experience. Our rehearsals were always rigorous and enlightening. In addition, I enjoyed attending Arturo's master classes, where he was consistently insightful and encouraging to student musicians. I often describe Arturo, himself, as a musical instrument, in that he uses a multitude of amplifiers, such as trumpet, piano or percussion, to project his music. His performances are extraordinary—from the scat singing to the jew's harp. I cannot imagine what the experience was like to be on stage with both Arturo and Dizzy!

Certainly, you will enjoy this delightful tribute book encompassing the special relationship between Arturo and Dizzy. The Germans have a tradition called "Gedenkschrift," which is the making of a book honoring a respected person. It is a celebration publication published posthumously as a memorial dedication. Although many of the photographs included are amateurish in nature, they do capture the moment and the immediate bond between Dizzy and Arturo. Thank goodness they exist. It is amazing that someone

On tour in Puerto Rico with Arturo's Band.

always seemed to have a camera handy. Furthermore, this volume also demonstrates how these musicians traveled to so many countries in such a brief time, and it documents the amazing receptions they had. Thank you to all who contributed photographs, time, efforts, and memories to this book.

Karl Marx Theatre, 1986.

Latino Plaza Jazz, 1986.

Europe, 1991, after defection.

Dizzy was talented, a true original, a statesman on an international stage, inspirational and nonpareil. He was one of the first musical celebrities to create a trademark for himself with unusual, self-appointed iconic looks. Dizzy's look was special, with his bent bell trumpet, distinctive hats—early on, black horned-rim glasses, mustache and goatee, and beret. Undoubtedly, his most distinctive feature became his inflated frog-like cheeks coupled with the bent trumpet. Dizzy, obviously, did not give in to popular opinions —he created new ones. Above all, he took pride in being a humanitarian. One of Dizzy's greatest achievements and contributions to music was not only the discovery, but the encouragement and promotion of Arturo Sandoval.

Robert Simon

Robert Simon
Winston-Salem, NC

A bibliography on jazz material can be never ending. The following articles and books are incorporated into the views of this book along with Arturo Sandoval's experiences. Specific references used for this publication, credits and other recommended sources for additional reading and viewing include:

1. Bebop, Scott Yanow, Miller Freeman Books, San Francisco, CA, 2000 - *chapters: 3,4,6 & 7*

2. Dizzy Gillespie and the Birth of Bebop, Leslie Grouse, Antheneum Books, NY, 1994 - *chapters: 6 & 7*

3. Groovin' High—The Life of Dizzy Gillespie, Alyn Shipton, Oxford Press, NY, 1999 - *chapters: 1,2,3,4,6 & 7*

4. The Life and Times of John Birks Gillespie, Donald L. Maggin, HarperCollins Publishers, NY, 2005 - *chapters: 1,2,3,4,5,6 & 7*

5. To Be or Not...To Bop, Dizzy Gillespie with Al Fraser, Doubleday Press, NY, 1979, revised publication, University of Minnesota Press, Minneapolis, MN, 2009 - *chapters: 4,5,6 & 7*

6. Movie: A Night in Havana: Dizzy Gillespie in Cuba, Chisma Productions and Cubana Bop Partners, USA, 1989 - *chapters: 5,6 & 7*

7. Recommended YouTube videos: Arturo Sandoval and Dizzy Gillespie - Jazz by adabergar, Dizzy Gillespie and the United Nation Orchestra, Live at the Royal Festival Hall, London, by Captain Joshie

8. Biographical Encyclopedia of Jazz, Leonard Feather and Ira Gifler, Oxford University Press, 1999 - *referenced chapters: 6 & 7*

9. Chano Pozo, The Original Conga, Latin Beat Magazine, Jesse Varela - *chapter: 7*

10. Chano Pozo, Allaboutjazz.com/php/musician - *chapter: 7*

11. Master of the Horn, Genius, Player, Jester by J. Brooks Shepherd, All That Jazz, May/June 1997 - *chapters: 5,6 & 7*

12. Jazz, Ian Carr, Digby Fairweather and Brian Priestley, Rough Guides, 2000 - *chapters: 6 & 7*

13. Afro-Cuban Jazz, Scott Yanow, Miller Freeman Books, 2002

14. Trumpet Kings, Scott Yanow, Backbeat Books, 2001

Dizzy, Stan Getz, Paquito D'Rivera and Arturo, 1977.

Arturo teaching Dizzy to play the guiro in 1977.

Dizzy's First Visit to Cuba

*"For me, he was, and is still,
the most musical trumpet player
that ever lived."*

May 17, 1977, the first American cruise ship since the Cuban Missile Crisis in 1961 entered Havana Harbor for a two-day visit to Cuba. Among the passengers was a group of leading jazz musicians from America, including Dizzy Gillespie, Stan Getz, Fatha Hines (Earl Hines), Ray Mantilla, Daniel Amram, Ry Cooder, and several others. As these celebrities disembarked, a notably eager fan waited at the end of the gangway, desperately hoping to meet his hero, Dizzy Gillespie.

Arturo Sandoval spoke only Spanish, but he was determined to find a way to overcome the language barrier that separated him from his hero. In his own vivid words, spoken now in English with a rich Cuban accent, Arturo describes passionately the first time he met Dizzy.

"You know, a lot of people thought that Dizzy was in Cuba many times before 1977; but no, that was the very first visit. The way I found out about it was kind of funny. I knew a guy who worked in the musicians' union in Havana. We had known each other since we played in the Tropicana, the big nightclub. He had seen a notice of an American cruise, full of musicians, that would be stopping in Havana for 48 hours. It was kind of a secret, a state secret. It was kind of taboo that anybody should know about it, and was, you know, like everything in Cuba, very complicated. But that guy called me, and said, 'Arturo, I know you like Dizzy Gillespie very much, and you're a big fan and so on. I'm going to tell you a secret. Don't say that I told you, but he is going to come this afternoon on a cruise ship. They're doing a jazz cruise in the Caribbean, and they're stopping in several countries, and they're going to stop in Cuba for 48 hours.' I said, 'WOW!' I couldn't believe it. I was so happy and I was crazy. I didn't know what to do. Then I found out what time the cruise was going to arrive in the Havana Harbor at the port, and I was right there waiting, by myself. At that time I couldn't speak any English at all— nothing, nothing at all—and it was funny because I was thinking, oh, my goodness, when I see him coming down the stairs I would love to say so many things, but I know I won't be able to say anything. And I felt very frustrated about that. But I was lucky because as soon as he got off of the boat he started to walk down the stairs, and I was waiting right there. I saw him, and I will never forget that impression, you know, to see a guy I admire so much. I had heard so many of his records, and he had already been my hero for many years before I met him.

I never heard any trumpet player or any musician that impressed me more than Dizzy. His recordings made the biggest imprint on my thinking long before I ever met him. He was mentally ahead of every musician around, and he was an innovator and a musical genius whose approach was completely beyond everyone at that time. Dizzy created a revolution in music as he completely changed the concept of playing and improvising, especially how to express an idea through an instrument in jazz. You see, Dizzy changed it so completely. It was only himself, and he was a virtuoso who had the capability to make it happen. Sometimes people have the ideas, but they have not mastered their instrument the way he did, and they cannot express the ideas the way he could. It is impossible to do what he did without the total command of the instrument, and there are no shortcuts as you must master your instrument. To play Bebop you cannot have limitations. You must enjoy the freedom to express ideas through your instrument without thinking about any physical impediments. You must be in absolute control and be able to perform your ideas without struggling. Dizzy thought so harmonically, and was so deep in the changes, as he had so much knowledge of the changes, whether on trumpet or piano, and combined that with an unusual sense of rhythm. He played completely different. And some people wrongfully place a little more credit on Charlie Parker's part in the creation of Bebop because he died young. Dizzy put those ideas in Charlie Parker's mind and Dizzy was the creator of Bebop, and after 50 years we are still trying to figure out and learn how to play Bebop correctly. To be a good Bebop player, you need to be a quick thinker and cannot be slow in any way, and sometimes things happen so fast you have to think doubly fast to express your ideas in this way of playing. And Dizzy was the creator of that when the rest of the world was playing completely different. Before Dizzy, jazz was far more limited to the basics of harmony and rhythm with stricter rules. Around the splendor of Swing, Dizzy came out with this new way of improvising. And of course, like any innovator, a lot of musicians did not understand or accept his new concept because they could not process as it was far too much information for them to process. Amongst them, with all due respect, was Mr. Louis Armstrong, who was one of the greatest pioneers of the whole age. But in the beginning of Bebop, he was one of the vocal ones who refused to understand Dizzy. He was hard on Diz, unfortunately, and that was a common mistake a lot of people made, including me. I remember the first time I ever heard Miles Davis and I said: "What is that?" I thought, that guy does not know how to play the trumpet, and I was completely wrong, of course. And later on, I understood it was a different style and way of playing. At that time, I was very deep into classical music, and that was a mistake a lot of other people made, too. Dizzy was a very musical person, and one of the things that influenced me the most was how enthusiastic and how hungry he was to learn something new and help us understand his ideas. Diz always had time to explain his ideas and learn anything from anybody, as he was always like a young student, starving for new information, and that was an inspiration for us all. You know when your hero has that kind of attitude,

ARTURO
SANDOVAL

22

On the SS Norway, at the time the largest ship in the world, during Arturo's first cruise with Dizzy along with a large group of jazz guys.

During their first meeting in 1977.

and he was a role model, it inspires you to follow and learn more about music. For me, he was, and is still, the most musical trumpet player that ever lived. I would like to say Dizzy was the most musical trumpet player that walked the face of the earth.

And then, finally, he came down the stairs of the boat, and I was in front of him that day and I couldn't say a word! But a guy who was walking behind him, who happened to be a Latino guy (Ray Mantilla), who was in that band playing percussion, talked to me in Spanish and said, 'May I help you? Do you want to say something to him?' I can't remember exactly what he said, but I said, 'Sure, of course. Can you help me? Do you speak English?' And he said, 'Yeah, yes, yes, yes!' I said, 'I would like you to tell Dizzy that I am a big fan of his and am here to be in his service. Whatever he wants to do or whatever I could do for him, please just let me know, and I would love to, you know, help him in any way.' And this he told Dizzy. And I said, 'What did he say?' And then he translated it. The only thing he said was, 'Has he got a car?' I said, 'Yes, I've got a little car there.' At that time I had a '51 Plymouth. We had just, me and my father, painted it with a brush of asphalt (tar) diluted with gasoline. You know, it was black, thin, and horrible; we painted it with a brush. The car looked terrible! And I said, 'Yes, I've got a little car. What do you need?' And he said, 'I want to go to the neighborhood where the people play percussion and those kind of things. I want to meet people, I want to meet musicians, I want to see the city. This is my first time over here.' I said, 'Sure, I'm the

guy.' And it was funny because the passenger door of the car was broken, and he had to get through the driver door to get inside. And then, I'll never forget, he asked Mantilla to ask me if that was a Russian car, and I said, 'No, no, it is an American car. This is a Plymouth, 1951.' He said, 'Wow, I thought it was Russian!' And then I started to show him the city, the whole city, up and down. And then I brought him, of course, to the Pogoloty, where I knew all of the people had played Afro-Cuban music for many years. At that time, so far I had never told him that I was a musician, not even a trumpet player, no, forget it. I never mentioned that. I never mentioned that I was a musician at all. I was embarrassed to say that.

I brought him to the neighborhood where the people played the Cuban drums and danced for him. He had a little camera, and he was shooting everything. He would turn around every once in awhile and would open his mouth and his eyes wide like he didn't believe what he'd seen. He was very excited. And once in a while, he'd say, 'Look at that woman. She looks like my aunt! Look at that one. He's like my brother!' And he was very impressed, because he knew a lot of Cubans, he said, over the years, but he had never been to Cuba before.

That evening the Cuban government, or Ministry of Culture or something, put together a kind of jam session with a band I was a member of; Irakere was the name of the band. They said they were going to bring all of the American musicians over to get together with us to meet each other

and play, and so on and so on. I said, 'Okay, good—beautiful!' They didn't know that I was hanging with him all day long. Because at this time, we were not permitted to interact with foreign people without a government permit. Anyway, I played the game and said, 'Yeah, yeah, we're going to meet tonight. Yeah, beautiful!' So in the late afternoon, I brought Dizzy and the others back to the cruise ship because they didn't have a hotel room. They were staying on the boat. He said, 'Tonight we're going to have a jam session with the band.' Through a translator I said, 'You are? That's very interesting—great!'

Then when he came back there that evening, he came backstage. Our band was warming up, you know, playing around, and I was warming up with the trumpet. When he saw me holding it in my hand he couldn't believe it. He looked puzzled and asked, 'What the hell is my driver doing with a trumpet?' Somebody said, 'No, he's a trumpet player.' He said, 'No, he's my driver, I know the guy. He's my driver!' And then we started playing together, and so on. Of course, I knew a bunch of his licks, especially his signature phrases and things, and I had a place in the chart where I played a long solo. I'd do the fermata and in the end I'd do the cadenza. And I started to play a bunch of Dizzy's things. He was laughing, and he was having a great time, and even tossed up a white tablecloth like he surrendered. From that day on, I believe we connected very easily, very, very well.

...that's a blessing from God, especially when you have an opportunity to meet your hero, that's something unique. We admire them as idols and heroes in every career. Some people never have an opportunity to meet these people. Dizzy was so accessible, he was so open and easy to talk to and to get along with. This was something organic.

In the end of the show, we played together, also with Stan Getz and a couple of others. You know who was on that cruise, too? Fatha Hines, the very, very famous pianist; Ray Mantilla was the guy who played percussion; Ron McClure, bass player. A group of great musicians.

Man, of course, I couldn't believe it. Because it was the first time in my life I had the opportunity to play with American musicians. I was so impressed and so excited. I was trying to listen and hear everything, and trying to learn as much as I could in a few minutes."

In New Jersey, 1979. Arturo on congas, Dizzy, Rodney Jones on guitar.

Arturo's First Performance in the United States

"Man, that made my heart twice the size of my body. I couldn't believe it."

Irakere, a politically correct name that did not specifically indicate "jazz," was formed in 1973 by several members of the Orquestra Cubana de Musica Moderna to blend traditional Cuban music with conventional jazz. Irakere was the first Castro-era jazz ensemble permitted to tour abroad and to record. Founding members included: Arturo Sandoval, Paquito D' Rivera, Chucho Valdes, Jorge Varona, Carlos Averhoff, Carlos Del Puerto, Carlos Emilio Morales, and Jorge 'el nino' Alfonso. In 1978, Irakere received a Grammy Award for "Best Latin Album." Executives from Columbia Records went to Cuba and signed Irakere to a recording contract. Columbia then brought them to the U.S. to have their premiere in Carnegie Hall.

"The very first concert we ever played in New York was at Carnegie Hall. We landed in New York in June of 1978, and they put us on a bus, and we headed straight from the airport to the sound check in Carnegie Hall. We played the second half of the concert. In the first half of the program there were two different trios: the Mary Lou Williams Trio and the Bill Evans Trio. When we were in the dressing room before the concert, there were so many famous musicians who came to welcome us. Then one guy came up to me and said he was Maynard Ferguson's manager and that

Maynard was on the way over and should arrive any minute. And he wanted me to know that Maynard would like to play something with me on the program. I said, 'Oh, my goodness, that's gonna be something tonight. This is gonna be a magical night.' Can you imagine the very first day ever in America and we are playing at Carnegie Hall, and in our dressing room are all these legends that we dreamed of meeting for so many years? Finally, Maynard arrived, and right away he was looking at my old horn, which was falling apart—I had a rubber band holding the water key. He was laughing as he looked at my horn and opened up his case and showed me his trumpet. He asked me if I would like to try it, and I said yes.

I played a couple of notes and he asked me if I liked it, and I said, 'Yes, of course, it is a great horn, really beautiful.' Maynard said, 'Okay, it's yours!' He gave it to me two minutes after we just met! He continued and said, 'It's yours, but let me use it to play with you at the end of your set and afterwards I'll give it to you.' That night in the first row, there was Dizzy, Stan Getz, Mario Bauzá, Maynard Ferguson, Toots Stillman, Tito Puente—oh, my goodness, a lot of great, great musicians. I couldn't believe it. Being there was Heaven. I said, 'Wow, this is too much!' It was a

ARTURO SANDOVAL

29

New York City, Carnegie Hall dressing room, 1978. Irakere and many other notable musicians including Dizzy, George Butler, David Amram, Alfredo Rodríguez, Mario Bauzá, Carlos Del Puerto, Arturo, Carlos Averhoff, Enrique Pla, Maynard Ferguson, Stan Getz, Bruce Lundvall, Paquito D'Rivera, Carlos Emilio Morales, Jerry Masucci.

lot of pressure for us because we were not used to playing in front of those big guys. So later on in the show, Stan Getz and Maynard joined us for the last couple of tunes, and we jammed, that was too much already.

A couple of days after the premiere, I went to Dizzy's house and he gave me one of his horns, too. The very first night was Sunday night. Then Monday there was the Thad Jones and Mel Lewis Big Band that used to play in the village every Monday night. And a friend of mine there brought me to the village to see them. Wow! What a hell of a band! And then when I met him, I brought my little horn. I had it under my arm when we had interviews with Thad Jones. He was a very nice guy, very nice. He asked me, 'Hey, you brought your horn?' I'd say, 'Yeah, yes.' He'd say, 'Go over there and play with us!' Then he'd pull up a chair and put me in the section there, and I'd play all night long with the Thad Jones and Mel Lewis Big Band. That was the second night. I said, 'Wow, man. This is a country where I would love to spend the rest of my days!' You know, from that day on, and even before, I was trying to figure out how to come here. I felt like all those things had a lot to do with me. You know what I mean? I thought

Jorge Varona, Arturo, Dizzy, Maynard, Carnegie Hall, 1978.

this was the place where I had to live to be able to hang with those people and listen to this music, and learn about this music. At that time I still could speak very little English, very little. A little bit. It was funny.

When I came back to Cuba, I had Maynard Ferguson's trumpet in one hand and Dizzy's horn in the other. Can you imagine? I had those two horns in my hands at the same time, and I was not going to let them go for anything. I was so happy and inspired—it was all just so amazing—like a dream.

One year later, we had another good opportunity, as CBS brought us back to the United States and put us on a bus for a three-month tour. We were the opening act for Stephen Stills, the great guitarist, who was doing an R&B act (later with Crosby Stills Nash & Young). That was something, because the audiences were expecting rock music of some kind, and here we were a bunch of crazy Cuban guys playing Cuban music. They did not respond well because they were expecting something else. They were saying, 'What the hell is that?' But anyway, it was good exposure for us, and we traveled all over the U.S. I'm telling you, in those days, when I started to meet people around New York and then later in Chicago and different cities, when I would get introduced to someone or something, they'd say, 'Oh, you're Sandoval? Yeah, I know about you.' I'd say, 'How?' They'd say, 'Yeah, Dizzy was here last month, or last week, or two month ago, whatever—and he was talking about you.' Man, that made my heart, you know, twice the size of my body. I couldn't believe it. Can you imagine? Dizzy was talking about me with people in different cities in America. That was very rewarding for me because that gave me a lot more inspiration and desire to keep practicing and to believe in what I was doing. He gave me the ultimate confidence.

Dizzy's second visit to Cuba, which was in 1986.

Dizzy's Second Visit to Cuba

Dizzy's next visit to Cuba was not until 1986, and at that time Arturo had his own group called the Arturo Sandoval Band. Arturo tried to put together his own group when Paquito defected in early 1980. The first two years were very difficult because the Minister of Cultural Affairs said if Arturo left Irakere to start a new group, no support would be given. No instruments or permits for performances would be granted; however, Arturo did it anyway, forming the Arturo Sandoval Band with a premiere on Valentine's Day, 1981.

"Even when we met, and I couldn't talk to him directly, we looked into each other's eyes and we said things. I felt that."

Not to be overlooked, Mario Bauzá (born Havana, 4/28/11; died NYC, 7/11/93) made several contributions to Dizzy's career, including Dizzy's entrée to Cab Calloway's band and the development of a mutual curiosity and a deepening interest in Afro-Cuban jazz. Perhaps more importantly, he introduced Dizzy to Chano Pozo.

Chano Pozo (born Havana, 1/7/15; died NYC, 2/12/48), a most astonishing and fascinating percussionist, had a natural ability to add excitement and distinctive rhythms to any variety of performance. He, more than any other musician, inspired Dizzy to combine Afro-Cuban music with jazz. Chano co-wrote some pieces with Dizzy that were premiered at Carnegie Hall in 1947. Chano Pozo is considered to be one of the greatest conga players and drummers in the history of jazz.

"But I've got to tell you something. Talking about a language barrier, when Chano Pozo went to New York with Mario Bauzá, who brought him from Cuba to New York in 1946, and then Mario introduced Chano to Dizzy, Chano never learned how to speak a word of English — nothing! He lived a year and a half in America, composed all that music with Dizzy, and he never learned how to speak anything in English.

Dizzy was always talking about Chano Pozo or told a story of something relating to Chano... for him it was very important because, even the first time and every time he went to Cuba, he always asked me where was the Chano Pozo statue or Chano Pozo's street or Chano Pozo's park, or something. He was expecting that people were really going to pay tribute to him in some way. And then I said, 'No, no,

Chano Pozo.

Dizzy's second visit to Cuba in 1986.

Dave Valentine, Dizzy, Arturo, 1986, second visit.

there is no park, there is nothing.' Many of the people here didn't even know who Chano Pozo was. And it's true still, you know. A lot of people don't even know about him at all. He came to America in 1946; he died in 1948. A very few of the very, very old musicians knew him a little bit. Dizzy expected that a lot of people in Cuba should have known about Chano. He was really very disappointed about that. He was expecting more reverence for Chano's name in that country. And Dizzy and Chano never did communicate through English or Spanish. They communicated only through music. That was the only way they could talk. Dizzy described in a video how they wrote the piece 'Manteca'

Dizzy, Alfredo Peres and Arturo at National Hotel in Havana, 1986.

together. It was so funny how Chano would show Dizzy what he thought the trombone should do, what the saxophone should do, and the bass, and the rhythm, and so on, without words—Dizzy was writing down everything...music is the only international language. It's the only language everybody understands. We can communicate with each other easily. If you speak the language of music, we're going to understand each other. Dizzy said, 'Even when we met, and I couldn't talk to him directly, we looked into each other's eyes and we said things. I felt that.' And also, I believe when you want to understand someone, you will.

Dizzy pretending to be a hotel employee and looking for his time card, 1986.

Castillo del Morro in Old Havana, 1986.

At the Havana School of Music, 1986.

National School of Art, 1986.

Dizzy taking it to the streets while filming A Night in Havana.

With Chano Pozo's sister - Petrona Pozo.

I don't know how, but you say, 'Wow, I want to understand what he said.' After that, I was just so happy to have the opportunity to be around him and learn. And when he talked, I was dying to understand everything he said.

Also, it was very interesting to go and meet members of Chano's family. My bass player's wife at that time in Cuba, her second name, or last name, was Pozo. She was related to him. I think she was a niece or something of Chano Pozo. So she helped me to find out where Chano Pozo's sister, Petrona Pozo, was living. We went there to meet her. We went to her little apartment and so on, and Dizzy was very depressed because those

Petrona showing a family picture.

people really lived in an extremely poor little apartment. He was depressed about that, and he started to ask people how he could help to arrange some royalties or anything belonging to Chano to go to these people in Cuba, his sister and their relatives. They lacked a lot of necessities. That was Dizzy. He was very interested in trying to help. And I think he did do something. He talked to the people at Capital or BMI or one of those companies, and arranged something so that money could be sent to these people.

Dizzy and Arturo improvising together, 1986.

En route to meet Fidel Castro, 1986.

Karl Marx Theatre, Havana, 1986.

*Reminiscing for an interview about communication.
through music as a universal language.*

Karl Marx Theatre, Havana, 1986.

At the keyboard together.

Outside and open to anyone, Havana, 1986.

At the Havana School of Music, 1986.

At the Karl Marx Theatre in Cuba, 1986, during filming of A Night in Havana.

In Old Havana, 1986.

Dizzy's room in the National Hotel in Havana, 1986.

Dizzy meeting Arturo's family for the first time—Marianela with his younger son Tury at age 7. In the background is Gilberto Valdes. Dizzy remarked that he sees now why Arturo stayed in Cuba.

Gilberto Valdes, Angel Cisneros, Dizzy, Arturo, Marianela and Tury, 1986, in the lobby of the Karl Marx Theatre.

Marianela's father, Juan, Dizzy, Marianela and her oldest son Lionel, in 1986.

Lionel Matthew Lartus, Marianela's son from her first marriage.

Arturo and Marianela's house in Miramar.
Marianela prepared for Dizzy, Lionel and Tury
traditional Cuban food, 1986.

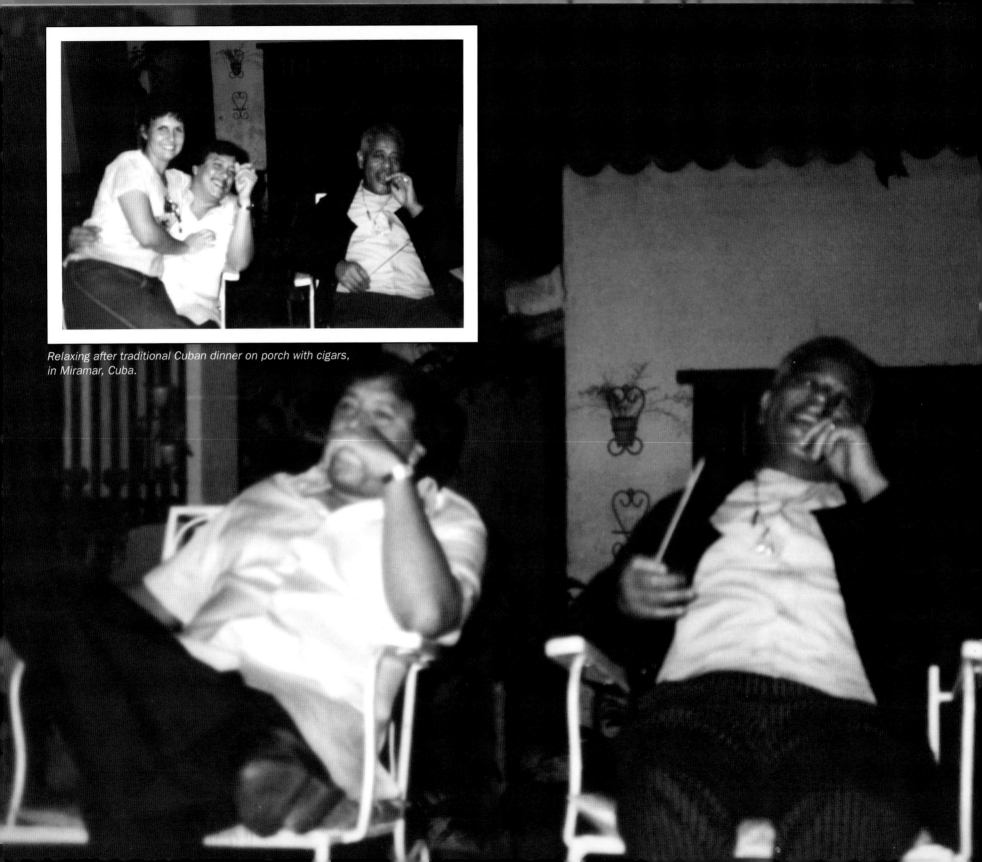

Relaxing after traditional Cuban dinner on porch with cigars, in Miramar, Cuba.

In Arturo's house in Miramar. Dizzy explaining the importance of the piano as the foundation of all music, 1986.

Dizzy meets Cira Arocha, Arturo's mother, and Arturo Sandoval, Sr., 1986.

Dizzy's caption reads: AS with "Cecil B." Gillespie, February, 1986.

During second visit to Cuba, February, 1986.

Third visit to Cuba, 1990. Dizzy requested a meeting with Fidel Castro.

Dizzy's Third Visit to Cuba (1990)
Dizzy and Arturo Meet Castro

"Dizzy was a very intelligent person. I know for sure he realized how crazy about power and how much of an egomaniac Fidel Castro was."

(Arturo was president of the Plaza Jazz Festival in Havana – He called Dizzy and invited him to perform in the festival. This brought Dizzy back for a third time in February, 1990.)

Although from two politically distinct countries and totally divergent eras, Dizzy and Arturo shared many things. Both men grew up in a poor, rural environment lacking any formal music education. Self-taught trumpeters through their midteens, each had a rare affinity for the piano and an ability to grasp intriguing harmonization. As their careers advanced, both of them felt the pain of discrimination; however, despite any prejudice encountered, each man became a universal champion of music and blasted the trumpet to unprecedented new highs. One man was born in a Democracy. The other man labored for creative freedom under the domination of Communism and the dictatorship of Fidel Castro.

Third visit to Cuba, February, 1990.

"Dizzy's third visit to Cuba was very interesting. He spoke to me one day and said, 'I would like to meet Castro.' I thought, uh oh, here's another mission. And I said, 'You know, I can ask a couple of people and tell them what you would like to do, but I cannot promise you anything.' So I talked to a couple of people, and one of them was a secretary. I knew her from a long way back, and she was the secretary of the Minister of Culture in Cuba. She said, 'Okay, I'll go and talk to the Minister. Maybe he can arrange something. I'll let you know.' Then she called me the day after and told me Castro was going to meet Dizzy tomorrow at 3:00 or 4:00 or something in his office. I said, 'Wow!' He was happy to meet Castro because, for a lot of people, Castro was, well, Castro still is kind of like a mystical figure or something. And Dizzy remembered in 1960, Castro going to Harlem and staying in a little hotel there, trying to do politics with the black people with the black community in New York. They met there very briefly. Castro forgot about that when Dizzy

Dizzy playing while Carmen McRae watches. Jazz Festival in 1990.

mentioned it. Finally, we got to his office and sat down there. It was like five, six people, we were in there together. Dizzy really demonstrated to me how he really wanted to help me because he knew how frustrated and isolated I was in Cuba. Every time he had the opportunity, he tried to do something to give me a break. And that day, I'll never forget, he started to talk to Castro, and the only thing he was talking to him about was me. Dizzy would say, 'You see this guy over here? This guy is the greatest trumpet player...,' and so on. And Castro's answer was, 'Would you like to come back and spend some vacation time, do fishing with me, and you can bring your family?' and so on. Dizzy said, 'This guy is amazing...' He said a lot of good things about me. But Castro never looked at me directly. Not even once, like he was ignoring what Dizzy was saying. And his reply

all of the time was, 'Come here and vacation.' He said, 'Do you like cigars? I'll give you a couple of beautiful cigars.' He always answered with something different, constantly trying to avoid the subject. That was my meeting with the dictator. The sonofabitch!!

Maybe Dizzy was a little confused, like a lot of people are. But Dizzy was a very intelligent person. I know for sure he realized how crazy about power, and how much of a egomaniac, Fidel Castro was. He's one of those guys who doesn't care at all about what anybody else could think or feel. Castro goes by his own thing, and the only thing he cares about is what he thinks of something. This man is very involved with himself. His ego is bigger than earth.

I've got one photograph I'd have to look for with the three of us: Castro, Dizzy, and me, with Dizzy on one side and me on the other side. He put his arm over Dizzy's shoulder, and he'd turn around to me like he was giving me his back. Yeah, he liked to give me his back. And now I'm so happy because I don't want his arm over or touching my body in any way. I've never touched him. I don't want that kind of vibe near my body."

Dizzy, Fidel Castro, and Arturo. Notice his back to Arturo.

Marianela Sandoval and Dizzy with Angel Cisneros, who was responsible for many of the five-star hotels in Cuba, February, 1990.

Marianela and Dizzy hanging out in 1990.

Dizzy talking with Chano Pozo's sister, Petrona, on his third visit to Cuba in 1990.
Petrona was the youngest of five siblings, wrote a tune herself, and was the only family member to survive.
Photo by Arturo.

The "Suzuki Team" with Tury, Arturo and Dizzy in front of Sandoval's house in Miramar, Havana, Cuba.

Villa Barlovento resort, again in 1990, father and son.

"Look out below." Havana, February, 1990. Photo by Charles "The Whale" Lake.

Returning from a motorcycle ride with Arturo in Miramar, Cuba, 1990.

Barlovento resort in 1990 while Dizzy was attending the Jazz Plaza Festival. Photo by Charles "The Whale" Lake.

Villa Barlovento, getting ready to jump, 1990.

ARTURO
SANDOVAL

Villa Barlovento, after the jump, 1990.

London airport, the day Dizzy welcomes Marianela and Tury. Arturo said at this moment, "We are not going back."

Arturo Defects While on Tour with Dizzy

*"Dizzy, you know what? I've got a surprise for you.
I don't want to go back to Cuba."*

In 1986, Arturo co-starred in a full documentary, A Night in Havana, about Dizzy's second visit to Cuba. The film clearly demonstrates that the relationship between the two musicians was deeper and more meaningful than that of mentor and protégé. In 1988, Dizzy hired Arturo as a feature musician with the United Nation Orchestra, which was touring extensively throughout Europe. During a tour of Greece and Italy in 1990, Arturo became determined to retain the freedoms that he had enjoyed while on tour away from the suffocating tyranny of Fidel Castro. He confided to Dizzy that he and his family planned to defect to the United States. This was a risky and traumatic experience for everyone involved, but Arturo was convinced that this was the only way to guarantee his family a secure and promising future. The way Marianela and Tury were able to join Arturo for part of the tour was a savvy negotiation on Arturo's part. He pointed out the money he had earned for the Cuban government on previous tours and that Marianela had been in England three months prior without any issues. Adding Tury into the mix was another

docudrama.com

hurdle to jump, and again, it came down to the government receiving a lot of money from Dizzy for a six-month tour. How could Arturo be expected to go without seeing his family for so long? He then received a special permit for Marianela and Tury to join him for two weeks in London.

"I didn't want Dizzy to worry, or have a preoccupation about any of it. I never mentioned anything until my wife and son arrived in London and they were safe there. I talked to them, and when I knew they were okay, then I talked to him. I said, 'Dizzy, you know what? I've got a surprise for you.' He said, 'What?' I said, 'I don't want to go back to Cuba.' He said, 'What? What are you talking about?' I said, 'Yes, my wife and son are in London already, and this is it. I'm not going back to Cuba.' And then that evening we had a reception in the ambassador's house in Greece, in Athens. We talked to them a little bit. They said, 'Okay, let's get together tomorrow morning in the Embassy.' So we went to the Embassy in the morning to start to fill out all of the papers and questionnaires and things. When we got to the Embassy that morning in Athens, everybody recognized him. And he, unfortunately, I'll never forget, he fell in the stairs in the entrance of the Embassy and broke one of his fingers. And the first thing they had to do, before we met anyone, was bring someone with a first aid kit to do something about his finger. And then he asked for the Ambassador to arrange a meeting. I remember what he said, the Ambassador, at the end of interviewing me. He said, 'I think it would be good if you finish your tour. You finish your tour, and then on the last day of your tour, you go to the American Embassy and they're going to know about you.' I said, 'Okay.' Then three or four days later, we've got like ten more days, but three days later I was in Naples with Dizzy, and my wife called me from London in the middle of the night. She was desperate and crying because she found out the people from the Cuban Embassy were looking for her and Tury. They were looking for her and my son. They wanted to catch them and send them back to Cuba. I was in London a few months before when somebody from the Cuban Embassy shot a Cuban defector named Aspillaga in an alley. It was all over the media, all over the news. The British government expelled the Cuban Ambassador and First Secretary, and left a skeleton crew to run the Embassy for months until a new Ambassador could be appointed. I had the memory of those things very fresh in my mind when my wife called. All of our dreams would be dead. I went to Dizzy's room and I woke him in the middle of the night. And I said, 'Diz, I'm sorry. I cannot finish the tour. I must go now.' And I told

him about the situation with my wife and son. Thank God, they were in a place where nobody knew where they were. A very good friend of mine had a little stone house in the middle of the countryside in England, and they were there. Nobody knew where it was. They were kind of safe.

But besides that, I was very worried. Because if they got my family, then they had me, you know, because I would never leave them behind. I was to operate the whole thing, the whole plan. So I woke Dizzy up in the middle of the night. We talked about the whole situation. He said, 'Okay, I'm going to call the White House. I've got a bunch of numbers here these people gave to me when I was on Air Force One. I went down to Namibia, in Africa, for the liberation with a bunch of people from the government, including the Vice President (Dan Quayle), who gave me these business cards.' All of those people, important people in the White House, respected and admired Dizzy. And they said, 'Dizzy, if you ever need anything, please call us any time.' He said, 'They told me if I needed anything I should call them.' And so he called the White House. Whoever answered the phone there in the White House wanted to talk to me, and he asked me a couple of questions. He had me explain the situation over the phone, especially about Marianela and Tury, and the state they were in there in England. I said the Cubans were looking for them, and I was very worried and very nervous about that. And he said, 'Now when I finish my conversation with the American Ambassador (to Italy),' we were in Italy at the time, a small town in the countryside,

Arturo and Pete King, who was the owner of the Ronnie Scott Club in London. He helped Arturo and Marianela so much when they were planning to leave Cuba. Pete and his wife Stella hid Marianela in their house for more than a month while Arturo was on tour with Dizzy.

Last United Nation Orchestra Tour, 1990.

'he's going to call you right back. He said to stay put in Dizzy's room for the call. Then you explain the whole thing to him, and he's going to have some instructions for you.' And then the Italian Ambassador called me back right away. I explained everything to him, and he said, 'Jump on the first plane in the morning and come to Rome. I'm going to be in the airport waiting for you.' I got on the first plane to Rome. Some people from the Cuban Embassy in Rome were waiting for me in the airport. The only thing they didn't know is the American Embassy car could get into the runway right there. And a couple of people from the Italian police went to the plane to pick me up. As soon as I got off the stairs of the plane, I got immediately into the American Embassy car. I never went into the airport building in Rome. We drove straight to the Embassy to fill out all of the papers and answer all the questions. Then the Ambassador asked me why I was still so worried. I explained to him the horrible situation with my wife and son in England. And he said, 'Okay, we're going to call the Embassy there and try to arrange something.' Not long after they told me, 'Do not worry. There is a car picking them up. They're going to bring them to the American Embassy in London right away. They're safe already.' Man, I felt a big relief when I heard that they'd picked them up already in the car, and they were on their way to the Embassy. I said, 'I think we made it!' I feel, in the end, we would have gotten political asylum, of course. Though I felt at that moment, without Dizzy's help, we might not have all made it safely.

After days of anguish, Arturo, his wife Marianela, and son Tury were safely reunited in New York at LaGuardia Airport. Eventually, many members of their family (including Lionel Lartus who was Marianela's son from her first marriage) were permitted to join them in America, where they all settled in Miami, Florida. Initially, Arturo and Marianella planned to live in New York, but their self-appointed and adoptive father, Dizzy, was concerned that his pseudo grandson, Tury, would flourish best in a different environment. So they moved south. A Home Box Office movie, *For Love or Country, The Arturo Sandoval Story*, recounting Arturo's flight to freedom, was released in Fall of 2000 and starred Andy Garcia as Arturo Sandoval and Mia Maestro as Marianela. The film received four Emmy nominations. In 2001, Arturo received an Emmy Award for Best Musical Underscore for a Motion Picture for his original compositions in the film. The movie captures the essence of the father-son and musician relationship between Dizzy and Arturo.

...to the Los Angeles Premiere of

ANDY GARCIA
FOR LOVE OR COUNTRY
THE ARTURO SANDOVAL STORY

Wednesday, November 8, 2000

7:30 pm Screening

DIRECTORS GUILD OF AMERICA
7920 Sunset Boulevard
Los Angeles

Party and Performance to follow at

THE HOUSE OF BLUES
8430 Sunset Boulevard
West Hollywood

Check in for the screening and the party will be at the DGA.
Shuttles to the House of Blues will depart from the DGA.

RSVP ABSOLUTELY REQUIRED
For Reservations, please call (310) 201-9367
Reservations will be taken on a first come, first served basis

This invitation is strictly non-transferable.

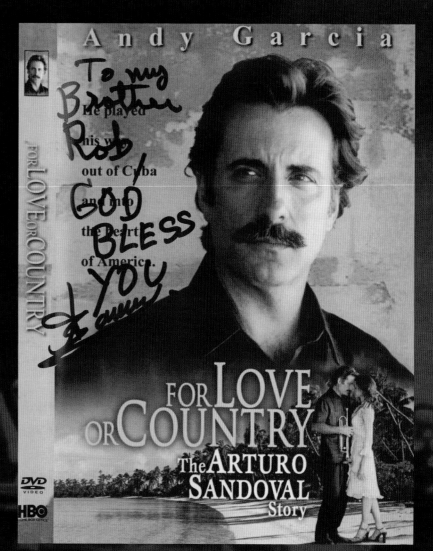

Andy Garcia as Arturo Sandoval.
Mia Maestro as Marianela Sandoval.
Courtesy Home Box Office

"There have been throughout history important artistic collaborations between mentor and protégé that have inspired great music: Aaron Copland and Leonard Bernstein are prime examples. Dizzy Gillespie and Arturo Sandoval were meant to be. Dizzy's genius both as an instrumentalist and as an arranger/composer live forever in his music and are carried on with true inspiration in the artistry of Arturo Sandoval. Like Dizzy, Arturo is a man of true genius, not only with his horn but also as an accomplished pianist, arranger, and composer. His love of Dizzy is in every breath he takes and every note he hits. I have had the extreme pleasure of playing Arturo in a film on his life, which explored their relationship, and I can tell you firsthand his love and devotion to Dizzy is heartfelt, lyrical, and magical. Dizzy is remembered by all, but his soul, his music, his love, lives on inside his adopted son, Arturo. Blow man, blow!"

Andy Garcia
Los Angeles, CA
7/2/13

Arturo with Andy Garcia during filming of For Love or Country.

Portrait of Dizzy Gillespie, New York, NY, ca. May, 1947.

Dizzy Atmosphere

by Robert Simon

"Dizzy" Gillespie, with his frog-like cheeks and neck inflated just shy of exploding, and his trademark bent trumpet with the bell pointed upwards, redefined the technical limits of the trumpet. He is considered, along with Charlie Parker, to be the founder of Bebop—a new style of jazz with melodic leaps and unusual intervals, all at an accelerated tempo. With his unique vision, he became a significant bandleader, a consequential composer and resourceful arranger, an extraordinary scat singer, a master entertainer, and one of the greatest jazz musicians of all time.

Dizzy was also one of jazz's first important educators. He had a natural flair for encouraging emerging musicians, always willing to explain or demonstrate his innovations to them. With his depth of chord structure, he had a natural tendency to force notes that seemed out of place into the perfect place. A self-taught musician, he had rapid and furious reflexes, which included fast runs, enormous intervallic leaps with unprecedented slurs, and explosive ideas capped off with vast and clear high notes.

Unlike most other beboppers, Dizzy enjoyed singing, dancing, telling jokes, and horsing around with the audience. Besides all of his showmanship, he was a cultural ambassador and a humanitarian. He led one of the first Bebop orchestras and established that bop was not limited to the small combos as commonly believed. Determined to feature Latin percussion regularly in his orchestras, he demonstrated original ideas and pioneered the development of Afro-Cuban jazz.

John Birks Gillespie was born in 1917, the last of nine children in a poor family living in Cheraw, South Carolina. His father, an amateur musician, died when John was only ten years old. John worked as a manual laborer in the fields around Cheraw. He quickly realized he hated picking cotton. He started playing trombone at age twelve, but could not reach the full slide positions, so he switched to trumpet a year later. He took to the trumpet right away and got local gigs playing, and even dancing, which he loved. At age sixteen, he was awarded a football and music scholarship to the Laurinburg Institute in

Dizzy with older brother Wesley in Cheraw, SC.

North Carolina, a co-educational high school and college for gifted black youths. However, he ceased participating in football because of the risk of having his teeth knocked out and thus affecting his trumpet career. He played in the band while at Laurinburg Institute but, due to a limited music staff and his already advanced performance abilities, it appears he did not receive much in the way of a formal music education. He became frustrated and dropped out of the Institute and found his way to Philadelphia, where his family had moved. Later in life, the Laurinburg Institute would award him an honorary high school diploma during a tour with Ella Fitzgerald.

Dizzy as a student at the Laurinburg Institute, second row, far left. Courtesy of the Frank "Bishop" McDuffie, Chair, Music Dept., Laurinburg Institute.

with a recording session, and in a short time, Hill's band toured Paris and London, providing Dizzy the opportunity to see the world and build a musical foundation incorporating a variety of influences. This was a big break for Dizzy. Upon his return to New York in the end of 1937, his forward-moving career came to an abrupt halt when he ran into a 90-day waiting period with the New York Musicians Union. In order to keep playing, Dizzy would duck and weave his way with out-of-town gigs with a low profile until the waiting period was over. It was on one of these trips where he met and later married (1940) the most stabilizing force in his life, Lorraine Willis.

In 1935, while living in Philadelphia, John developed his own original style of playing as well as a stronger knowledge of harmony. He joined the Frankie Fairfax Band, where he was first nicknamed the "Cheraw Flash." Fellow trumpeter Palmer Davis (Fats Palmer) dubbed him "Dizzy," due to his sense of humor, constant clowning and dancing all around like a dizzy cat. He soon moved into Roy Eldridge's old position in Teddy Hill's big band, originally emulating Eldridge's sound. Eventually Dizzy's musical curiosity broke the mold as he became a risk taker by experimenting during his solos. Most musicians (and audiences) of the time could not comprehend his innovations. It started

With his own style emerging, Dizzy developed his un-traditional playing in late-night jam sessions all over New York City. These sessions usually took place in the middle of the night after the evening performances were over. Though Dizzy was known for clowning around, behind his humorous wit was a musician with the capacity for inventive thought and quick understanding. It was soon apparent that Dizzy had a natural aptitude for stretching musical ideas into an original and desirable dimension. It was also at this time that Dizzy first met Mario Bauzá, who would not only introduce him to Afro-Cuban music, but who soon became a much-needed father-like figure to Dizzy. Eventually, Teddy

Late teens, John Birks, then was called the "Cheraw Flash," posing before his trek up north just prior to being nicknamed "Dizzy."
Courtesy of Jeanie Bryson

Portrait of Dizzy Gillespie, 52nd Street, New York,
NY, between 1946 and 1948.
William Gottlieb Photography
Courtesy of the Library of Congress

Charlie Parker and Dizzy in the 1940s.

Dizzy's Big Band at the Orpheum Theater in Los Angeles, late 1940s.

Portrait of Dizzy Gillespie and Charlie Parker, Carnegie Hall, New York, NY, ca. October, 1947.

(L to R) Lucky Thompson, Dizzy Gillespie, Charlie Parker, and Billy Eckstine, Pittsburgh, PA, 1944.

EXIT 2

EXIT 1

Hill's Band gigs came to an end and so did Dizzy's regular paycheck. He freelanced for about a year. Then Mario, so impressed and fond of Dizzy, called in sick to a gig with Cab Calloway and suggested that Dizzy walk on as a substitute. This was the biggest break of Dizzy's career, as Calloway's band was the hottest gig going. He played in Cab's band for two years until an unfortunate misunderstanding took place.

Dizzy was featured in several of Cab's recordings. While stifled musically by the straightforward arrangements played by Cab's band, Dizzy did learn a great deal about discipline. Cab would not tolerate drug use, alcohol, or sloppiness in appearance, all of which were all too common among the bands and orchestras of the 1930s and 1940s. Although his style appeared to be clearly defined already, Dizzy constantly experimented in Cab's band. Rarely pleased with this maverick behavior, Cab eventually fired Dizzy after mistakenly accusing him of throwing spitballs during a performance. Another trumpet player, Jonah Jones, was actually the guilty party, but instead of straightening out the situation, Dizzy allowed his infamous temper to flare and a fight ensued, which ended with Dizzy cutting Calloway in the buttocks with his pocket knife—a pocket knife that decades later would become a gift to Arturo Sandoval.

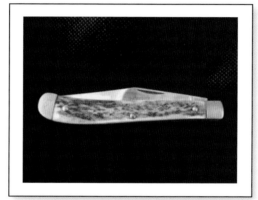

Dizzy's pocket knife as used on Cab Calloway—a gift to Arturo.

Dizzy moved forward and did some lightning-fast improvisation experiments at gigs with different rhythm sections, which turned into the roots of Bebop. In 1940, Dizzy met and shared these innovations with Charlie Parker, who also had many original ideas. Together their contributions formed the foundation of Bebop. Parker, who was heavily addicted to drugs, had a genius that stubbornly persisted with a distinct style of musical phrasing. This, coupled with Dizzy's sense of rhythm and knowledge of harmony, changed the heartbeat of jazz forever. They worked together from time to time and eventually recorded in the mid-1940s. During the early 1940s, Dizzy moved around from band to band, performing for Lucky Millinder, Ella Fitzgerald, Duke Ellington, Coleman Hawkins, and several others. He wrote many arrangements for these bands as well as for Jimmy Dorsey and Woody Herman.

Dizzy became a member of Earl Hines's band, a group also featuring Charlie Parker, Sarah Vaughan, and Billy Eckstine. This job represented another forum for planned Bebop. During this period, Dizzy wrote his most famous composition, "A Night in Tunisia." Soon afterwards, he led a Bebop combo with Oscar Pettiford before joining an orchestra that Billy Eckstine was forming. Many recordings took place, and

Portrait of Ella Fitzgerald, Dizzy Gillespie, Ray Brown, Milt (Milton) Jackson, and Timmie Rosenkrantz, Downbeat, New York, NY, ca. September, 1947. Courtesy of the Library of Congress.

Dizzy with John Lewis, Cecil Payne, Miles Davis, and Ray Brown between 1946-1948.
Photo by William P. Gottlieb.

before long Sarah Vaughan recorded a vocal setting of "A Night in Tunisia" under the revised name "Interlude." This version quickly grew to be a standard with all of the major orchestras.

1945 proved to be a banner year for Dizzy. It was at this time that his career really began to gel and things fell into place. Many of his own original classic Bebop charts were recorded, often with Charlie Parker, including "Hot House," "Shaw Nuff," "Groovin' High," "Dizzy Atmosphere," "Salt Peanuts," and "Tour de Force." This year also saw the formation of Dizzy's first big band, although this band would eventually fail when audiences found his music radical and tough to dance to.

At age 28, Dizzy Gillespie formed a second big band. Successful for several years, the band was a forum for many budding young greats such as Thelonius Monk, J. J. Johnson, Yusef Lateef, and John Coltrane. A wonderful band addition, Chano Pozo helped Dizzy introduce Afro-Cuban percussion to the Bebop culture, and before

long, "Cubop." Dizzy recounted, ..."I immediately contacted Mario Bauzá to see if he could get me a drummer and he introduced me to Chano Pozo, and from that moment on it was kicking butts! If anybody in the world knew Cuban music, Chano Pozo did." (quote from *A Night in Havana*) Tragically, Chano Pozo was killed a year later; but the influence of his Cuban rhythms stayed with Dizzy forever and inspired an even greater affinity for Cuban music and musicians.

1947 was highlighted by a concert in Carnegie Hall and several concerts in Europe. Many of Dizzy's contemporaries were critical of his music and some thought it was absolutely tasteless. In 1950, he downsized his big band to a small group that remained extremely active through the mid-1950s. Dizzy's mix of music now included some R & B as well as Bebop. In 1953, at Massey Hall in Toronto, Canada, Dizzy, Charlie Parker, Bud Powell, Max Roach, and Charles Mingus performed together during one of the greatest Bebop concerts of all time. This concert was considered by many to be a monumental event in the history of jazz. It was perhaps the last time Dizzy performed with Charlie Parker.

James Moody (sax), Chano Pozo (congas), and Dizzy, 1948. Frank Driggs Collection.

Portrait of Dizzy Gillespie, Downbeat, New York, NY, between 1946 and 1948.

Dizzy demonstrating the concept of Bebop in the 1940s.

Portrait of Milt Orens, Mary Lou Williams, Tadd Dameron, and Dizzy Gillespie at Mary Lou Williams's apartment, New York, NY, ca. August, 1947.

Portrait of Dave Lambert, John Simmons, Chubby Jackson, George Handy, and Dizzy Gillespie in William P. Gottlieb's office, New York, NY, ca. July, 1947.

Portrait of Dizzy Gillespie and Georgie Auld, Downbeat, New York, NY, ca. August, 1947.

Portrait of Dizzy Gillespie, Downbeat, New York, NY, ca. August, 1947.

Portrait of Tadd Dameron, Mary Lou Williams, and Dizzy Gillespie in Mary Lou Williams's apartment, New York, NY, ca. August, 1947.

Portrait of Dizzy Gillespie, Famous Door, New York, NY, ca. June,1946.

Portrait of Dizzy Gillespie, New York, NY, ca. May, 1947.

During 1954, Dizzy started using a trumpet with the bell pointed upwards after an accident where someone bent the bell to his horn. He liked it that way, and it became his most physically identifying characteristic. It also allowed him to project a more acoustically pleasing sound in clubs while creating new visual excitement. He continued his output of recordings throughout the decade, and by 1956, soon after Charlie Parker's death, he formed a new big band that was funded and promoted by the State Department for two years under the auspices of

Dizzy playing his trumpet, December 2, 1955. Photo by Carl Van Vechten.

President Eisenhower. After this, Dizzy focused mostly on quintets, but on many occasions he would assemble big bands when called for. He was often asked back to his ambassador and statesman role for cultural missions.

By 1960, Dizzy was revisiting the Latin sound he so enjoyed in the 1940s. His repertory expanded to include pieces featuring South American and African rhythms, many of which were recorded live in Carnegie Hall in 1961. The rest of the 1960s found Dizzy focusing mostly on Bebop. With bop as his core, mixed with Latin jazz, Dizzy also occasionally recorded funk-oriented music for several different labels. He greatly enjoyed performing, teaching,

Jazz trumpet greats Louis Armstrong and Dizzy Gillespie performing "Umbrella Man"

Tremendous parallels exist between Dizzy and Louis. They both are credited with creating unique trumpet styles, self-imposed iconic personas and development of unique musical languages. Both knew how to clown around on stage and constantly reinvented themselves decade after decade. Of course both were commercial successes as well as musical mavericks.

Portrait of Dizzy Gillespie, New York, NY, ca. May, 1947.

and inspiring others to perform. He remained a strong attraction for concert promoters, continued to be the happy consummate entertainer, and in 1968 once again led a big band.

By 1974, he was under contract with the Pablo label to record into the early 1980s. Throughout the 1970s Dizzy toured with many of the greatest performers. He occasionally played with Clark Terry, Roy Eldridge, and Harry Edison, and together they became known as "the Trumpet Kings." He also organized mature Bebop quintets and succeeded in shaping his old ideas of Afro-Cuban

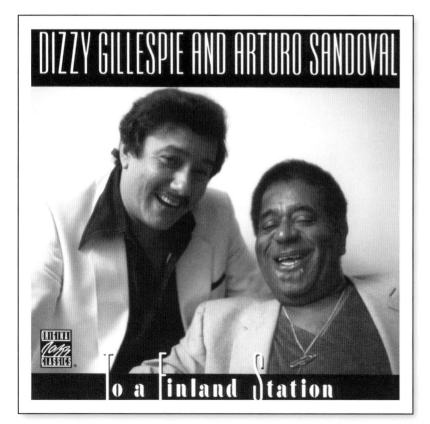

music into a final form. It seemed as though Dizzy was busy playing everywhere with everyone. His performances still included lots of clowning around, dancing, and great humor on stage.

After receiving great acclaim at the 1977 Montreax Jazz Festival, Dizzy traveled to Cuba, where he discovered Arturo Sandoval and Paquito D' Rivera. This fateful meeting marked the beginning of a new direction for the Cuban musicians. They both eventually moved to the United States. At age 65, in 1982, Dizzy recorded "To a Finland Station," considered by many to be one of his last significant recordings. He chose the great Cuban trumpet virtuoso, Arturo Sandoval, to share in the glory of the five original works recorded at this session. Arturo had played a taxing three-set gig that evening and Dizzy surprised him, saying he lined up a recording session with some locals late that same night. They worked until 6:00 am, producing illustrious solo after solo in this quintessential recording. Sandoval would go back to Cuba for another decade before defecting to the United States with Dizzy's assistance.

Dizzy's last big band was the United Nation Orchestra, an extremely Latin-oriented group that toured extensively and featured Dizzy as the international statesman of jazz. He was always concerned with the cause of world peace, and this gave him the opportunity to bring together many different cultures. The band showcased an allstar line-up of musicians including Sandoval, D' Rivera (who conducted

In Europe, warming up before a performance with the
United Nation Band in 1990.
Photo by Dany Gignoux.

the band in later years), Ignacio Berroa, Slide Hampton, Giovanni Hildalgo, James Moody, Airto Moreira, Danilo Perez, Mario Rivera, Claudio Roditi, and Steve Turre, among others. These musicians could execute anything Dizzy wanted and he was able to stand back and take pleasure in featuring them.

Photo by Dany Gignoux, Washington, DC, 1990.

"Yet another birthday."
Photo by Dany Gignoux, Washington, DC.

Even in his later years he continued to remain active, performing with symphony orchestras as well as playing and acting in a film called "Winter in Lisbon" in 1989. For his 75th birthday in 1992, Dizzy made his final recordings in New York surrounded by many of his favorite musicians during a two-month residency at the Blue Note in Greenwich Village. He ended his recording career with a 20-minute version of "A Night in Tunisia," nearly 50 years after it had originally been composed. It was another happy time for Dizzy, who could still perform wonderfully. Shortly thereafter, the mood abruptly changed when he was diagnosed with pancreatic cancer. He died less than a year later on January 6, 1993. He was survived by his wife of over 50 years, Lorraine, a daughter, Jeanie Bryson, who is a jazz singer, and a grandson, Radji Birks Bryson-Barrett, all of whom he loved very much.

Dizzy's remarkable career remains inspirational to this day. He rarely gave in to the pressure of pop culture. Instead, he persevered by leading the jazz world with a vision and a style of his own, now recognized as the historical standard throughout the world. He wanted to be remembered most as a humanitarian. Throughout his colorful life, John Birks "Dizzy" Gillespie did it all. Our world culture, musicians and audiences for generations will grow due to his vision. "Everybody has an angel and for us Dizzy was our angel" (a joint quote by Arturo and Marianela).

Dizzy at a concert in Deauville (Normandie, France), July 20, 1991.
Photo by Roland Godefroy.

Finland, 1982.

Painting of Dizzy (artist unknown).

Photographer Dany Gignoux in her studio in Geneva, Switzerland. She had the vision and fortitude to shadow Dizzy in performance for years taking amazing pictures around the globe. Dany then produced a book entitled DG + DG in the 1990s. Some of the astounding photographs in the following pages come from her body of work. Others can be found on pages 108, 109, 113, 147 & 183. Photo by Rob Simon, 2011.

Dizzy, Milt Jackson, Ella Fitzgerald, Montreux, 1981. Photo by Dany Gignoux.

Cab Calloway and Dizzy in New York, 1988, after many years apart.
Photo by Dany Gignoux.

30th Anniversary of the Festival de Jazz Antibes Juan-les-Pins.
Photo by Dany Gignoux.

Dizzy and Terri Lyne Carrington. photo by Dany Gignoux

Dizzy and Toots Thielemans. Photo by Dany Gignoux.

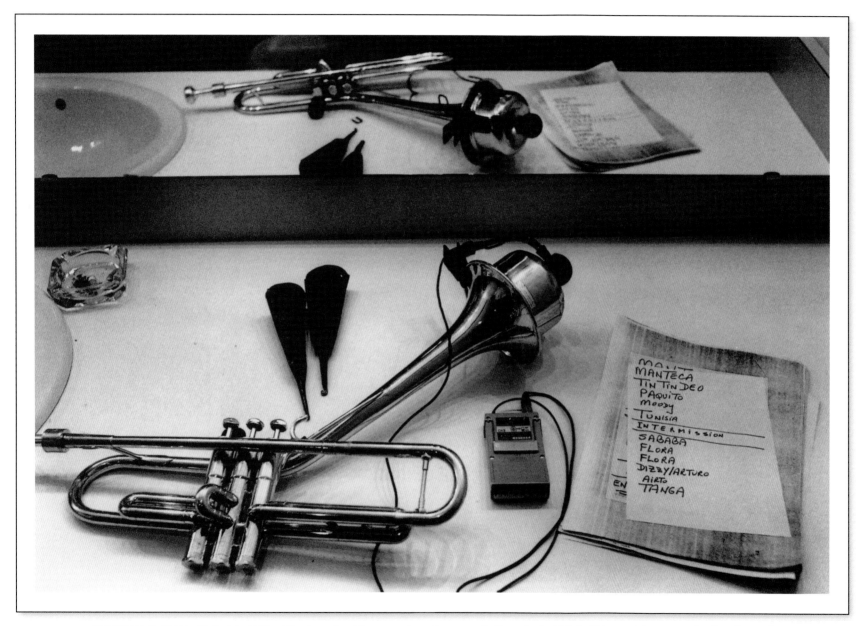

The Master's Tools - "I decided I liked the horn bent because I can hear a note the minute I hit it. This way I hear my mistakes faster."
Dizzy Gillespie in "American Way," 1990. Photo by Dany Gignoux.

Dizzy at the Palau de la Musica, Catalana, 1990.
Photo by Dany Gignoux.

Hotel Meridien, New Year Concert, 1991, Paris.
Photo by Dany Gignoux.

Dizzy in Geneva, 1991, Victoria Hall.
Photo by Dany Gignoux.

*Lorraine Gillespie unveils bust of her husband by sculptor Manuel Linarés
in the town of Le Cannet, in the South of France, 1993.
Photo by Dany Gignoux.*

Dizzy's statue in Cheraw, SC.

Chano Pozo

*"He was wild and musical, African and Cuban,
communicated with his eyes and his rhythm; there was
something forceful and reckless about him; and he was murdered."*

Born into poverty in Havana in 1915, Chano Pozo grew up in a world of criminal activity. His mother died when he was eleven, leaving him to learn at a young age how to survive on the streets. He flourished as a rowdy young delinquent until he luckily landed in a reformatory. While in reform school Chano learned to read, develop vocational skills, and focus on his natural ability of playing all types of drums. He found religion, was released back to his father, a shoeshiner in Havana, and even tried to take up that trade himself, but it just did not suit him. He played drums in Cuban and Nigerian religious cults, but made a living of sorts by selling newspapers. Chano's aggressive nature at hawking papers made him a standout and he was soon noticed by a racketeer who hired him as a collector and a bodyguard. It was an unusual combination: he was big and athletic for his age, a thug and a dancer, loved women and booze, and yet he was passionate about composing music.

People took note of Chano's compositions and his colorful nature as a streetwise rascal. His music won cash prizes in competitions; however, his goal was to land a job at one of the large hotels in Havana that catered to the tourist trade. He was denied this opportunity due to his dark skin and soon found himself a bouncer at a club and a doorman at a radio station. His intimidating physique and willingness to fight was, no doubt, a major asset to these positions.

Like Desi Arnaz and a few other notable Cuban musicians of the time, Chano moved to New York to establish a career as a conga player, singer, and dancer. He was fortunate to take part in a few recordings, as well as perform with different ensembles. His multi-rhythmic abilities set him apart and allowed him to adapt instantly to all the performers, including dancers. Chano played in several popular bands of the era and became friendly with Mario Bauzá, who introduced him to Dizzy Gillespie. Although Chano spoke no English, he made jazz history collaborating with Dizzy and became the first conga player to perform with a jazz band. It was Dizzy's vision to take the polyrhythms of African and Cuban music and combine them with American jazz. Chano became the conduit of the missing rhythms, rhythms that were the basic expressions and emotions of their ancestors. Dizzy said of

Chano: "He was a master at the two major sources of Cuban rhythms—the drums and the dance. He was putting Afro-Cuban music into jazz and I was attempting to put jazz into Afro-Cuban Music." (quote from "Night in Havana")

Chano Pozo made his debut of this new primal jazz format at Carnegie Hall, performing in a much-celebrated reunion of Dizzy Gillespie, Charlie Parker, and Ella Fitzgerald for New York's elite audience—an audience that no doubt was stunned by the added drum power and ancestral chanting.

Together, in their first year, Dizzy and Chano composed and recorded "Cubana Be, Cubana Bop," "Tin, Tin Deo," and "Manteca." These landmark compositions introduced Afro-Cuban jazz. History would reflect that Dizzy Gillespie and Chano Pozo were musical explorers and visionaries.

As fate would have it, Chano Pozo, his terrible temper ignited, humiliated and beat a man in public who had sold him some low-grade marijuana. Within a few hours the

man returned to the Harlem bar where the incident had occurred and shot Chano to death. A brilliant, truly original

Chano tapping out rhythm to Dizzy in the dressing room.

career shockingly came to an abrupt and gruesome ending. Chano, however, made such a lasting impression on him that Dizzy is said to have mentioned Chano and his rhythm in some way every single day for the rest of his life.

Belgium, 1989. Photo by Rob Miseur.

Reflections

"Without music, life would be a mistake."
—Friedrich Nietzche

Just as unique smells conjure up a past memory and bring it freshly to our minds, a particular sound or inflection of music triggers our deepest memories and brings the masters of the past to the stage once again.

No one understands this more than Arturo Sandoval, who, through his performances, honors the life of Dizzy Gillespie and celebrates the music he created. Every time Arturo performs Dizzy's charts, he feels close to Dizzy, even two decades after his death. For Arturo, the man and the music are one.

For Dizzy, life and music were one. He had the amazing ability to translate his unique thoughts into magnificent sounds. Dizzy knew that mankind instinctively communicates through music. The organized sound and silence punctuated by rhythm, which we recognize as music, resonates profoundly with everyone on earth. Dizzy celebrated that universal connection between all people that music and rhythm represent.

Dizzy was a master at improvisation, the art of performing without premeditation, and his influence is reflected in Arturo's jazz style. Dizzy's hunger to learn, grow, and teach created a legacy that he passed on to Arturo and that is evidenced by Arturo's own life and sense of musical responsibility.

There are very few original ideas—most things in life are variations on something that came before. Without repeated performance and recordings, our music and its culture would slowly fade away. It is through performance of our music that we protect the culture and heritage from which the music originated. Arturo says that "music serves the needs of the human emotions and we must keep the music alive!" His own dedication to this mission will hopefully serve as inspiration to the next generation of musicians.

It is Arturo's honor to lovingly acknowledge his deep appreciation for the gifts Dizzy provided to him and his family throughout the years, especially the gifts of friendship, confidence, and freedom.

GATE

AFTER 10 PM

Kentucky Fried Chicken Presents

SALSA
MEETS JAZZ
EVERY MONDAY
TONIGHT
ARTURO SANTOVAL
AND
MONGO SANTAMARIA
GUEST JAZZ SOLOIST
JON FADDIS

M.C. WKTUS 'PACO'

This Week
at the
Village Gate

Arturo, Dizzy, and concert promoter, Papo Coss, in Puerto Rico, mid-1980s.

West Berlin, Germany, with the United Nation Orchestra, 1989. Lower right-hand corner is pianist Danilo Perez. Photo by Uli Pschewschny.

Toronto, Canada, taken June, 1988. Photo by Barry Thomson.

Dizzy with John Lee in the background, Toronto, Canada, 1989. Photo by Barry Thomson.

With Jon Faddis in Toronto, June, 1988. Photo by Barry Thomson.

Dizzy conducting in Berlin. Arturo in background.

Discussing UN tour in 1991.

Life on the road.

UN Orchestra tour.

Bobby Carcasses, singer, and five trumpet players,
Jose Miguel Crego, Dizzy, Jorge Varona, Arturo, and
Juan Murguia.

Blue Note Club, 1980s, with Dizzy's band.

Arturo and Jon Faddis Tamoso Trumpetista de Jazz Northamericano. Photo by Marc Pokempner.

Europe, late 1980s, while on tour. Dizzy and Arturo share the same appreciation for fine cigars.

Arturo, Paquito D'Rivera, Dizzy in Paquito's family home.

S.S. Norway Jazz Cruise, 1992. Pictured are Arturo, Marvin Stamm, Dizzy, Red Rodney, and Jon Faddis.

Dizzy plays jew's harp as Maurice André listens. Photo by Dany Gignoux.

Dizzy and Maurice Andre' in Geneva. Photo by Dany Gignoux.

In Montreal, Canada, with guitarist Ed Cherry, 1991.

Arturo, Dizzy, and Jon Faddis in 1985.

(L to R) Jon Faddis, Harry Sweet Edison, Dizzy, Arturo, and Wynton Marsalis in the kitchen of the Blue Note Club, NY, circa 1985.

Jon Faddis, Arturo, and Dizzy.
Photo by Marc Pokempner.

Arturo and Dizzy at the Blue Note Club.
Photo by Marc Pokempner.

Photo by Marc Pokempner.

Arturo on piano at Blue Note.
Photo by Marc Pokempner.

Blue Note Club. Photos by Marc Pokempner.

Arturo and Dizzy at the Blue Note Club.
Photo by Marc Pokempner.

Arturo, Jon Faddis, and Dizzy at the Blue Note Club in NY, 1986. Photo by Delio Valdes.

With Poncho Sanchez in Italy.

In Italy with Poncho's group.

In Trinidad, Tobago, in 1989. Dizzy went to play with Arturo's band in the jazz festival there.

Competition to see who had the biggest belly while smoking.

Restaurant in Holland while on tour, early 1990s.

Arturo, Charles Lake, Dizzy, and trumpeter Claudio Roditti in Denmark, 1988.

Dizzy in 1988.

Dizzy in Paris.

Dizzy, Clark Terry, and Arturo in action.

Arturo, Clark Terry, Dizzy, and Claudio Roditi.

Clark Terry, Dizzy, and Arturo.

Dizzy watching Arturo cranking out the high one.

Clark Terry and Dizzy, Nice, 1983. Photo by Dany Gignoux.

Dizzy, Clark Terry, and Arturo.

Clark Terry, Charles "The Whale" Lake, and Dizzy.

George Benson, Arturo, and Dizzy in London at The Ronnie Scott Jazz Club, circa 1984.

At Ronnie Scott's Club in London with guitarist Joe Pass, Arturo, George Benson, and Dizzy.

Having a wonderful time taunting each other and playing it up for the audience.

Dizzy Gillespie
and
Arturo Sandoval
"A Night in Tunisia"

The Berlin Club, 1989, Toronto, Ontario. © 1989 Barry Thomson.

Photos by Barry Thomson.

The Berlin Club, 1989, Toronto, Ontario. © 1989 Barry Thomson.

Mentor and protégé very happy together.

A Night in Havana.

Ron Mathewson, Dizzy, Martin Drew, and Arturo in the Ronnie Scott Club in London.

Arturo, Dizzy, and Benny Barabara (trumpet player) in Canada, circa 1991.

Miscellaneous profiles of the master.

Carmen McRae and Arturo, 1990.

Cheeks in motion.

Autographed photo from Candido Camero to Arturo of a photo with Dizzy and Charlie Parker playing at Birdland in 1959 with Candido!

Toronto, Canada, approximately 1991.

Arturo with famous American swing band trumpeter Pete Candoli. He played with the bands of Woody Herman, Stan Kenton, and many others as well as having a significant studio career in movies and television.

With the great American jazz clarinet player Buddy DeFranco. He played with many famous groups including the Glenn Miller Orchestra.

Arturo and 14-time Grammy Award-winning producer Phil Ramone.
"I miss him terribly—he was so good to me!!!!" — AS

Quincy Jones conducting in The Hollywood Bowl with Arturo featured, 2011.

With Russian trumpet virtuoso Sergei Nakariakov.

Arturo and Dr. John the Night Tripper, American singer, pianist, and guitarist.

With American singer and songwriter Carole King.

Arturo with singer and song writer Natalie Cole.

Arturo with the great comedian, actor, musician, and producer—Dick Van Dyke.

On set with Steven Spielberg.

Arturo performing "Joy To the World" with astonished Danny Hutton and Three Dog Night with the Piedmont Wind Symphony, 2008.
Photo by Kevin Slusher.

Arturo autographing the soundboard of a Steinway Grand Piano.

Arturo in his home studio watching the Nicholas Brothers dance, LA, 2010.

100 lbs—no trouble.

Marianela and Arturo, Winston-Salem, NC, 2010.

Arturo at the keyboard in NC, 2010.

Jake Simon watches Arturo play Sureña in NC, 2010.

ARTURO SANDOVAL

229

Photos by Kevin Slusher and Rob Simon.

With radio executive and former President of ABC Radio, NY, Allen Shaw, prior to a concert, NC, 2010.
Photo by Rob Simon.

Arturo performed numerous times at The White House.

Arturo with President George H. W. Bush and Mrs. Barbara Bush.

Arturo with President Bill Clinton and Hillary Rodham Clinton.

Arturo and Marianela with Vice President Al Gore and Tipper Gore.

(L to R) President George W. Bush, Emilio Estefan, Gloria Estefan, Arturo Sandoval, Cristina Saralegui.

Arturo with Hillary Rodham Clinton.

President Barrack Obama, Michelle Obama, Marianela, and Arturo.

Arturo and Stevie Wonder on stage performing in The White House, May, 2012.

Arturo playing in a star-studded tribute to the songwriting team of Burt Bacharach and Hal David. In performance at The White House for the Library of Congress Gershwin Prize—the nation's highest honor for popular song. Other performers included Sheryl Crow, Michael Feinstein, Diana Krall, Lyle Lovett, Mike Myers, Rumer, Shelea, and Stevie Wonder, May, 2012.

Arturo and Stevie Wonder on stage performing in The White House, May, 2012.

Arturo with Burt Bacharach, Washington, DC, 2012.

Arturo and Marco Rubio in Washington, DC, May, 2013.

Friars Club honored Don Rickles with a lifetime-achievement award for comedy.
Along with Arturo are celebrities Bob Newhart, Bette Midler, Lewis Black, Billy Crystal, John Stamos, Regis Philbin,
Jason Sedakis, Bob Saget, Robert De Niro, Natalie Cole, Diana Krall, Kathie Griffin, Joan Rivers, and others, June, 2013.

At tribute with Don Rickles, June, 2013, at Waldorf Astoria, NY.

This was the front license plate of one of Arturo's cars.

At tribute with Don Rickles, June, 2013, at Waldorf Astoria, NY.